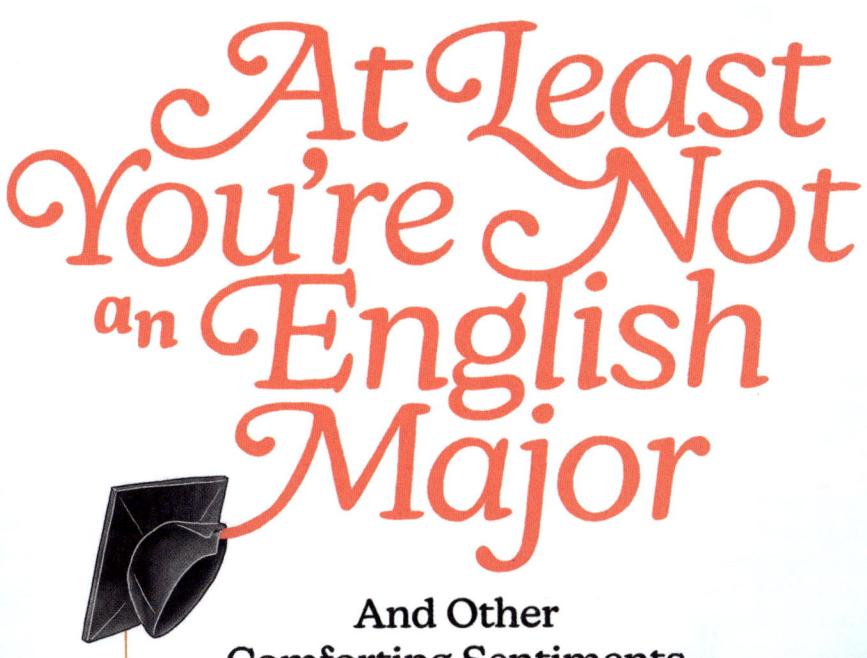

At Least You're Not an English Major

And Other Comforting Sentiments for the New Graduate

GLENN BOOZAN

Illustrated by Daniel Spenser

WORKMAN PUBLISHING • NEW YORK

Copyright © 2026 by Glenn Boozan

Hachette Book Group supports the right to free expression and the value of copyright. The purpose of copyright is to encourage writers and artists to produce the creative works that enrich our culture.

The scanning, uploading, and distribution of this book without permission is a theft of the author's intellectual property. If you would like permission to use material from the book (other than for review purposes), please contact permissions@hbgusa.com. Thank you for your support of the author's rights.

Workman
Workman Publishing
Hachette Book Group, Inc.
1290 Avenue of the Americas
New York, NY 10104
workman.com

Workman is an imprint of Workman Publishing, a division of Hachette Book Group, Inc. The Workman name and logo are registered trademarks of Hachette Book Group, Inc.

Illustrations by Daniel Spenser

The publisher is not responsible for websites (or their content) that are not owned by the publisher.

Workman books may be purchased in bulk for business, educational, or promotional use. For information, please contact your local bookseller or the Hachette Book Group Special Markets Department at special.markets@hbgusa.com.

Library of Congress Cataloging-in-Publication Data is available.

ISBN 978-1-5235-3318-3

First Edition February 2026

Printed in Shenzhen, China (APO) on responsibly sourced paper

Cover © 2026 Hachette Book Group, Inc.

10 9 8 7 6 5 4 3 2 1

For John.
*All the terrible decisions
I've ever made were worth it,
as they led me to you.*

Say **goodbye** to student life: so structured, safe, and warm.

Things won't be so **cozy** when you step outside your dorm.

Gripping your diploma tight,
you might begin to fret:

"What's my **future** gonna look like?

Where do I go **next?**

No more teachers, no more schedules, no more dining hall.

What if, when I'm on my own,
I spread my wings and . . . **fall?**"

Just remember this, more so than any platitude:

At least you weren't an English major.

Boy, those kids are **screwed**.

Oh, or **anthropologists**!
What do they even do?

Absolutely useless.
Thank goodness
that's not you.

Good luck finding work
if you picked ancient Greek or Latin.

What's the etymology of "Never gonna happen"?

Those who took **theology**
can pray to every god.

Still won't help a **single bit**
when looking for a job.

Most degrees in **art** lead to the unemployment line:

theater, painting, sculpture, dance, interior design.

Basket weaving, opera singing, poetry, or prose—

just be glad you had some sense and **didn't** study those.

*What if I **did** graduate with one of those degrees?*

... Please accept my heartfelt and sincere **apologies**.

Never mind the majors! Whatever path you take, you could have a PhD and still make huge mistakes.

Brilliant **Marie Curie** won awards for innovation

and **still** messed up by giving herself deadly radiation.

Galileo, he became the **best** astronomer.

All it ever did was make him quite **unpopular.**

So please take this heartfelt sentiment from history:

You could end up
dead or **broke**,
whatever your degree!

> A.I.'s taking all our jobs, the price of gas is NUTS. Global stocks are always CRASHING, EGGS are FIFTY BUCKS!

Well, touché. Our modern day can oftentimes . . . suck ass.

But! Have you considered it's way better than the past?

1300s Europe didn't rue
the price of **eggs**.

Kinda hard to do that
when you're **dying**
from the Plague.

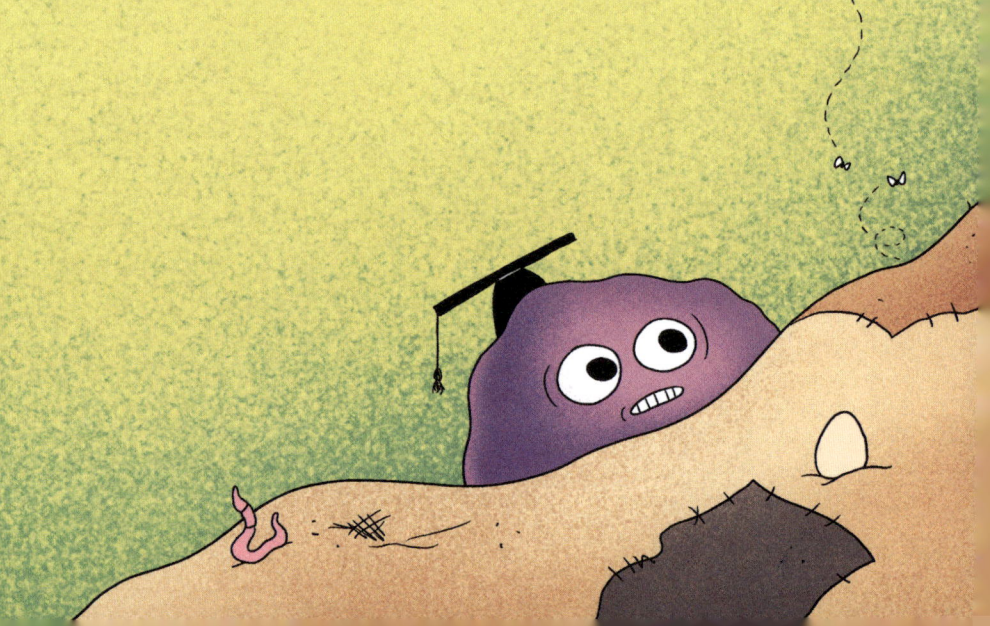

Robots coming for your job?
Quite scary, to be fair.

Would you rather be pursued
by prehistoric **bears?**

When you want to bellyache that **taxes** are too high,

just be glad there isn't **lava** raining from the sky.

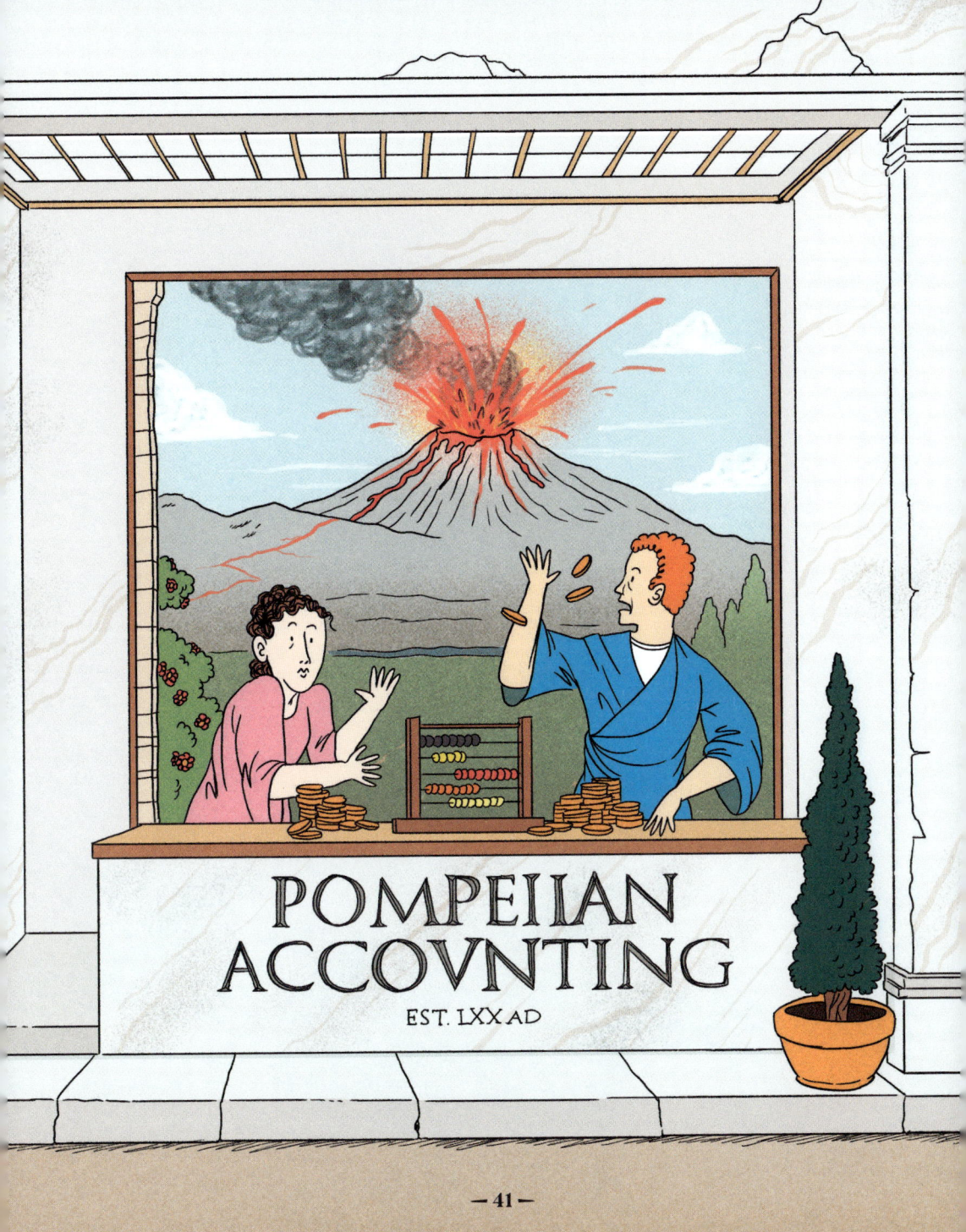

Logging in to LinkedIn
is **exhausting** nowadays.

Better than submitting
all your résumés in **clay**.

What about the Great Depression? Boy, **they** had it rough.

Maybe in comparison, your **problems** aren't that toug—

Billionaires don't pay their taxes, politicians cheat. And I'm supposed to take it on the chin and stay upbeat? Please just stop this optimistic singsong rhyming verse. Screw all your comparisons— in fact, I now feel worse!

Truthfully, **I must agree**,
    the world is sometimes shit.

I'm a **book** and I can see
how much is wrong with it.

That's why, after college,
    everyone gives you their **best**.

So, I think I'll change my tune.

I **don't** wish you success.

Instead? I wish you ups and downs.
I wish you highs and lows.

I wish your life **complexity,**
some **thorns** on every rose.

I wish for you **exciting stories,**
told among good friends.

I wish you **health,**
I wish you **wealth**
(the kind you cannot spend).

I wish for you a future full
of **marvel** and **surprise.**

I wish for you **adventures**,
in every shape and size.

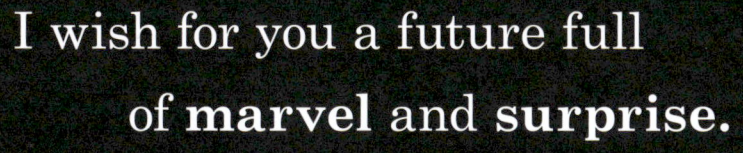

Follow every **wild** thing that makes your heart feel whole.

Do not let The Big Guys put a price tag on your soul.

Study "useless" disciplines,
go out and paint some rocks.

After all, dear graduate,
one life is all we've got.

No, it won't be easy.

Mankind can be **unfair**.

Gird yourself for times when you're depressed, alone, and scared.

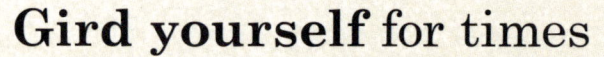

Everyone will give **advice** on what you ought to do,

but you **already** have the key. It's there inside of you.

So, when all that **anxiousness**
and **worry** start to mount?

Your major wasn't English . . .
and *that* is all that counts.

However . . .

If you **did** choose English,
and all this has you shook?

Hey, if all else fizzles . . .
   you can always write a book.

THANK YOU to my fellow classmates who helped with this group assignment: Brandi Bowles, Reg Tigerman, Rachael Mt. Pleasant, Rae Ann Spitzenberger, Lia Ronnen, Megan Nicolay, Beth Levy, Doug Wolff, MacKenzie Collier, Nicholas Teodoro, and the rest of the brilliant Workman team. To my friend, Dan Spenser: Thank you for illustrating this book before getting too successful to take my calls.

A special thank you to my parents for not complaining too much when it took me six years to complete a bachelor's degree.